COLISEUM

HÉCTOR CARRETO

Translated by Elvia Ardalani

Las Lenguas de Babel Collection
MEXICAN POETRY IN TRANSLATION

© Héctor Carreto, 2017
© Translation: Elvia Ardalani, 2017
© Libros Medio Siglo, 2017

All rights reserved. This book or any portion thereof may not be reproduced or used in any manner whatsoever without the express written permission of the publisher except for the use of brief quotations in a book review.

First Printing 2017

ISBN 13: 978-0-9864497-7-2
ISBN 10: 0-9864497-7-6

Cover Design/Diseño de portada: Victoria Selene Cantú
Original Drawing/Dibujo Original: Victoria Selene Cantú

This publication was made possible with the help of the Translation Support Program (PROTRAD) dependent of Mexican cultural institutions.

Esta publicación fue realizada con el estímulo del Programa de Apoyo a la Traducción (PROTRAD) dependiente de instituciones culturales mexicanas.

www.librosmediosiglo.org
mediosigloeditorial@gmail.com

Harlingen, Texas
USA

PRINTED IN THE UNITED STATES OF AMERICA
IMPRESO EN ESTADOS UNIDOS DE AMÉRICA

COLISEUM

Acknowledgements

To Dana Gelinas for giving me the title and for her corrections.

Thanks to Alberto de la Fuente for his comments.

I
[Inscription]

He gave himself in body and soul to poetry;

he was immortal while he lived.

II
[The Birth of Venus]

After being born from the foam,

dressed in her dress of drops,

the lips with the taste of seafood,

Aphrodite confessed to her poet:

"I do not believe in miracles or divine gifts;

I am as solid as the bread you bite,

imperfect like the rock or sleep,

my sex smells like sardine,

I like pearl necklaces,

light beer and to love without taking off my boots."

III
[Circus]

Strange awakening of Caesar

that afternoon in the middle of the Arena,

when he begged the Christian audience

that a gladiator put an end to his life,

that they release the lions,

that they would raise him to the highest cross.

IV
[The *Trojan* Horse]

That night, while Paris,

absorbed, polished his dart;

while Menelaus dreamed

with warm canvases behind the wall,

I slipped into Helen's bedroom

and, wrapped in a latex costume,

I managed to violate the blond doors.

V
[The Two Maecenas]

You are generous, Maecenas, with sycophants.
Peacock, do not boast the chest;
> that rich plumage is not yours.

The expenses you give do not jump out of your bag
> but from my taxes,

that assign you a salary to match your whims.

You are the patron of others; I am yours.

VI
[Caligula's Son-in-Law]

For judges of the literary contest

Caligula's son-in-law named the dogs of the Court.

They read nothing, it was understood.

Faithful snouts, they carried

laurel wreaths

to their owners.

Caligula's son-in-law looks satisfied:

To choose a judge, there is no instinct like his.

VII

[Caligula's Horse]

How outraged was the Senate

when Caesar's horse burst in

and occupied a seat.

They were right: a steed

does not fit in a donkey stable.

VIII

[Delikatessen]

I am very sorry, Hef,[1] not having attended

the feast of the rabbit[2].

I regret not to immerse myself in the foam of your Roman fountains.

It will be another time, Hef, when I spend the night

in the Grotto[3].

But tell me, on which knees did the dark glasses

sprig sit her golden buttocks?

What brand of sandals raised the tendons

of the Venus of Silicon? What tongues varnished

      her soles under the white tablecloths?

What rose-colored pig wallowed in the mud

      with the Fame?

Surely it was you, oh old goat.

---

[1] Refers to Hugh M. Hefner, creator and president of Playboy.
[2] It refers to the celebration of Playboy magazine in its 47th anniversary.
[3] Place where the most desirable *bunnies* on the market have made out.

I read about the bed for the big occasions,

where clusters of grapes are moistened and perfumed

      in the tender caves.

I close my eyes and see that bed plough into the sunrise,

towards the beach where it throws the naked bodies.

What, then, did the crew believe? Perhaps that like

      virtuous mothers, they would land on
unblemished soil?

They are not pharaohs, they are not saints, my good butcher.

You are not immortal either,

and fleeting is the fat free belly of the model of the month,

because although the juiciest females

      stick to the rigors of calories

and methodical practice aerobics and oral sex,

one day not even the least graceful of lovers

      will be his pair on the earthen bed.

(After yawning with your magazine,
I almost became a reader of chaste verses:
"The dry leaves, the intact rose ...")

IX
[She]

My owner, now, is called Prospero,

indeed, a rough man:

Does not understand, like you, high ideals,

his memory would never evoke The Metamorphoses.

But although he is not a rhapsode nor an academic

he knows how to distinguish between a woman and a mare:

he praises me with loving words

          that you denied me.

Tender, he caresses me,

brushes my hair

and proudly mounts me in front of everyone.

X
[Coliseum]

Oh, sublime Cleopatra,

owner of the Alexandria that we all carry inside

   -that land conducive to pleasure;

you, that do not find an equal

in the fight of ideas

nor in the kisses' combat;

You, who have never lowered yourself

   to look at this slave,

I give you these few words:

   I am unable to decipher hieroglyphics

and I am blind to the Latin of the conquerors

who enter and leave without a passport

through the sumptuous palace of your body.

I do not know the Greek spelling

but I understand the language of the hands.

Nor am I a Latin gladiator,

but if in the Arena we both released the tunics,

my rigid spear could make you my slave.

XI
[The Oldest Rat]

Like the oldest rat,

who eats, before anyone else, the new food

      to know if it is poisoned,

I must take the risk and be the first to try

      the pubis of that insinuating lady.

XII

[Nightmare]

She was more beautiful than two mares together, but even the devil would not dare mount her.

XIII

[Gymnasium]

You say, Claudio, that I do not have the Achilles biceps
    nor the thorax of Atlas?
You are right. Nevertheless,
I have a harder muscle,
that I do not exercise in the gym
but in the bedroom of the hungry woman.

XIV
[Burning the Eternal City]

This ode that I sign I dedicate to your consort,

the young caged lioness, Tyrannous,

the one with the parted lips.

Forgive me if I aroused your anger.

Is that why you canceled the publishers and supplements

        that published my verses

and ordered to burn my whole works?

Before so much inspired ash,

has your libido already been satiated?

You could not, however, turn on the fragile

        body of your beautiful beast,

nor could you turn it off.

Do you perhaps seek - as the vicious without a cure - more embers?

If you return some night without warning

and from the summit you watch a powerful fire,

it will not be, I assure you,

the cremation of my papyri

nor the burning of the Roman columns.

Something you call yours will burn in my arms.

Guess what!

XV
[The Alley of Miracles]

There never was a woman like you, Therapy "The One and Only":

Before you the blind man recovers the hot stripes of the tiger,

your firm fist throws the limping crutch into the river.

You ease, Therapy, anguish;

You purify cancer, you trade for bread

the stone that your soles tread.

But there is a secret, a number that does not come out,

a modest miracle that I could not applaud:

out of pity, Therapy, love me!

XVI
[The Obelisk]

The city

                ·fast ivy·

overflows beyond walls

and its entrails · temples,

villas, stadiums,

                host crowds.

My obelisk, however,

does not fit in the ass of Rome.

Instead, in your hidden little plaza,

oh, sweet Therapy, my needle moistens the Olympus.

XVII
[Virtual Reality]

Although you undress for me, Therapy,

I only touch you with my eyes.

Plato, my teacher, insists:

"It is impossible to possess, to touch Beauty."

With disdain I watch as your lovers

ride you up, down,

behind, through the mouth.

Naive: they ride on a silhouette.

XVIII

[Honors to Bacchus]

I will not uncork again a single bottle:

in order to lose me, you will only have to offer me,

appetizing Therapy,

the gift of your twin grapes.

XIX
[Love Sickness]

I do not care about a herpes infection

or other incurable damages.

It is the risk of desire, it is its mandate:

Drinking in your cup is, perhaps, my only chance

to put my lips on yours.

XX
[Drunkenness]

Well into the night

I can continue standing, drinking wine

that I begin when the afternoon is born,

and I testify how those who soon clashed their glasses

collapse.

Your eyes are two glasses that crash with mine;

a white sweat like nectar shrouds my body;

my senses, without a single drop, are disturbed,

my legs give up

and, even though I am an expert pugilist,

        I am the first to drink the soil.

XXI
[Twin Peaks]

To climb the Vesuvius, Prosper, you use all your effort.

Instead, I apply art to climb the Mount of Venus.

XXII

[Cronos]

Although the grandmother has acquired the finest gold watch,

time will continue consuming the old woman with the same appetite.

XXIII
[Cyclops]

Why do you watch me at all times
       -as I write, read
and when I bend or cross my leg?
Are you perhaps an entity of greater stature, obsessed
       in my most petty acts?
Listen: I'm not a hero
           at the top of any watchtower
nor do I lead ships with argonauts.
I'm just an unsigned editor,
           one more number on the payroll.
No one gave me a role in the tragedy.
I become invisible when I encounter Sophocles.

Go, eye without eyelid, return to your island:
              watch your goats.

XXIV
[Mythology]

Why didn't you ever tell me, mother,

that those fables you told me as a child

- about harpies, cyclops, gorgons-

   were only children's stories?

Why didn't you forewarn me?

Blind and without sword, little by little I got into a more ominous

   maze, where I still do not spell

   the face of the Adversary.

In these office halls

     I endure pecks,

my brain gets upset by the commands

     which jump off the cliffs,

my feet dodge Medusa.

Now I know: I am not that hero.

Adult, I have no return:

My sword?

I would have to look for it on the lost ground of childhood.

II
Funeral Occasion

You, funeral occasion, fiery reunion.
Pablo Neruda

I
[In the Tomb of Helen]

In life her beauty had no equal;
nor her cruelty.
Do not allow, grave,
the resurrection: because of her
many spilled their lives.
In their name
I beseech you, Mnemosyne,
make us forget her baseness
and give us enough memory
to praise her unparalleled eyes,
now in amphorae,
now in unhappy epigrams.

II
[The Blind]

Although he writes speeches,
Victoricus is illiterate:
he has not read his epitaph.

Victoricus is already deceased
and still does not know it.

III
[The Return]

What are you doing here?

Last week I wrote your epitaph.

IV
[Offer]

His own life came ·at a high price,·

his love for a cheap woman.

V

[A Tomb Without Inscription]

They will not place on your head

a bust similar to Dario's

or that of those wealthy senators.

Like the lost Argonauts,

an oar without a name will signal your grave

and perhaps only the woman who loves you

repeats your verses.

To a greater homage you cannot aspire.

VI
[Forever Cinderella]

Next to your newly sealed tomb

I leave you that sandal

That you lost at the dance

and that in the threshold you waited for

until the end of your days.

VII
[Petition]

Have pity for Victorious
　　　　-newly deceased-
who never wrote
a single graceful poem.

May a couple of memorable verses accompany him
　　　　　on his journey to the afterlife.
Be generous with the guild, Anonymous:
on his gravestone chisel the epitaph.

VIII
[Urns]

At the foot of your tomb I place,

like empty urns,

your high open shoes

for you to leave, when you wish,

to visit your night corners

or to step on those dance halls

or find on a new lap the flame.

IX
[Leonidas]

I congratulate you, Leonidas;
Your book was a sales hit.
No more debts.
Now the Armani
          and the Jaguar of the year,
could be yours.
You could travel to the confines of Europe
and acquire a villa
close to Sharon Stone's.

Pity, Leonidas,
that Fortune knocked at your door late
and you cannot even smell the flowers
that your fans have taken you to the crypt.

X
[Democracy]

Do they want to be chosen to take part in this anthology,

smile in the group photo

and find a chair at the end of the year dinner?

Do not worry: everyone

will have a place, sooner or later,

in this cemetery.

XI

[Octavius' Epitaph]

Octavius, master of this house, has died.

He is survived by his cats.

Who should drink the glass of milk?

XII

[With Novenius, in the Republic of the Dead]

During my stay in the city of the dead
        I stumbled upon the old poet Novenius.

Jostling as a young man, the old man used me as a shoulder to cry on:
        "I've only been five years away from my empire
and already my verses, those sullen walnut trees,
are no longer sold in bookstores;
in the library, nobody looks for my file;
my young widow, with another surname,
cannot recite completely one of my verses.
        (Hey, who warms my throne?)
The heir dodges the path that bears my name
and the very rascal loudly repeats words of minor poets.
What a stupid and miserable century!

It is a consolation that you, Anonymous, have not written
    anything worthwhile;
you will never know what oblivion means for an immortal.
"

III
Satellites

The Conquest of Space

Even distant, the stars are like your eyes.

"Another expedition to heaven,"
the media announces without emotion.

The crew is not adventurous.
The oars are keys
that the astronauts press, the electrical engineers,
the politicians of Space.
(They do not seek sacred treasures
but a less burning truth).
For them Jupiter, Saturn, Venus and Mercury
        are not gods
-they do not influence our emotions; -
they are only points where you can nail a banner.

When will a poet navigate
        on a NASA spacecraft,
that sings to the war unleashed by two opposites

and the unprecedented beauty of such distant landscapes?

It does not matter:
> Homer founded the myth of the West

without having ever seen the walls of Troy.
> (With sealed eyes he witnessed the descent

of the gods).

I sing to the constellations

without knowing how to read the maps
> and without having wrapped myself
>> in the mantle
>>> of any galaxy.

I have traveled farther, beyond the exact sciences:

yesterday I approached the enigma of your open eyes.

Astronaut Warning

On my journey around the Earth

thousands of miles from you, Therapy,

I warn you: "behave well."

Even if you want to, you will not hide;

I will watch your actions from the mast.

From the Moon, the Emperor Confesses

Of all my colonies

the one I prefer is this moon

because from there I look out to the world

like someone who, without being seen,

peers behind a sphere.

From this point I can frame

the carnival in the harbor

and the parade of the carriers

towards the Middle East,

I can enjoy the sunset over the islands,

chase after the sparkle of some eyes

and, from a turning key,

the fluttering in the sunken coin.

I can follow the multiplication

in the mirrors of the ladies in waiting

and I can, especially, contemplate

the exclusive spectacle of your body

throw itself on another beast.

I am that beast, right, Therapy?

Right, I am the beast?

IV

Infections

*But write with humor your Roman poetry,
and may life be portrayed in it.*

Marco Valerio Marcial

My Poem, That Beast

My poem is nourished by human beings.

It does not matter if they pant

or if they lie on gravestones.

Bite the high nipple,

        that after the infection it will become ode;

lick the blood of the martyr,

        which will take the form of elegy.

Listen to the bustle of the swings

and even if it drinks from the poisoned vessel, it will come out unscathed.

When I sleep fumble in the dumpster of my dreams,

and when I open my eyelids, I stumble over some gnawed bone

        or with the intact corpse of my father.

Sniff the impure flower: dampen the clitoris.

When satisfied

it becomes word

        in verse

              in poem.

Masterpieces

Before the pride of Melos,

that extracted Venus,

                    not from the foam

but from the intractable stone,

you, Lord, gave light to Therapy,

more graceful in her movements,

with a livelier gaze

        and warmer arms.

However, unlike that famous

and quiet deity,

one day Therapy's clock

will lose the last grain of sand.

Lord:

        If you can make such a graceful creature *see* me,

I promise you to give her a breath

of eternity in the odes that I write to her,

so that her grandchildren admire in her

>your work.

If you convince her, Lord,

I will put your signature at the bottom.

The Site of Troy

I will not write anything that my eyes do not see:
Cyclops, lotophages and laestrygonians will not nest

                                                in my
verses.
The continent that goes from your foundations to your dome

            will suffice to found a mythology.

I will not convey the songs aloud,
a raphsode's resource, more beautiful than certain
(from language to language the truth changes its nature.
Where is the bed, still warm, that unleashed a drama?)

I will be faithful to the facts:

On the map I will stick a pin in that bar
where, anxiously, the garments sought to flee

           from our bodies;
another one in the hotel room where I was dazzled

           by the gold of your nipples.

I will back up my verses

to avoid the confusion of the archaeologists

that will try, in five thousand years, to decipher my metaphors;

that they do not extract a false Troy,

or when opening a tomb where we never slept

        they confirm: "They are Paris and Helen."

I will be faithful to the facts:

My avid, nervous verse,

will confess how my pupils woke up

        with the singing of your sandals,

how, under the spell of your lips,

I became a bird.

Be wary, reader, of the press,

the voice of radio and television images;

the truth is on this diskette, CD

or printed poem that I put before your eyes.

Infections

"Poetry rises in you, Anonymous,
like grapes in the noble vineyards.
Instead I am fertile writing memos,"
You confess to me not without envy, Victoricus.
"Right, I say, we are both desk moles.
We enjoy, however, five free minutes a day,
      and in those blinkings,
in dark cubicles, we received sweet visits
which transmit us incurable diseases:
the popular Timoclea lavishes you,
the unsociable Muse infects me."

Dante Points Out

"Who are they, Dante, those who in the bathroom

are grading Poetry? "

"Your sin is being naive, Anonymous; don't you recognize them?

That one intends to possess her for thirty pesos;

This one seeks to show her off in cocktail parties.

To preserve her purity,

that one over there submerges with a diving suit;

that one measures her charm by her measurements;

the other one invokes her with dubious words of sorceress;

this other one has good intentions,

but he lacks the talent to dance to her rhythm.

They are the chosen ones to form a peculiar anthology,

with great virtues

                without literary value.

The Poet Scolded by the Muse

"Before her hair, the wind

was unable to get entangled.

Intact, her lips remain.

Only the light-cameo- fixed the memory,"

those were the verses I wrote thinking of Her.

After reading them, the Muse dialed my number:

"Why do you describe me with words of epitaph?

According to my hand mirror, I'm not dead

        nor am I a statue.

Do not want me to resemble your mother.

Are you sick or what wrong

forced you to change your poetics?

Do you hold a tomb in the Rotunda

     of the Illustrious,

in the National College,

     or do you savor a lifetime diet?

Listen to me: do not write anymore as an abstracted geometer,

in words that sound like clanging crystals,

and never paint a battle like a honeysuckle bouquet.

Trust your instinct: that your lips refer with pride

        my talent in dancing, my love of wine.

Brag to the reader of my legs on a crazy bike,

of the sweaty encounters, whose fruits

        are your epigrams.

Do not hide that we have differences.

Between the muse who quarrels with you and the one who sleeps on a canvas,

do not hesitate: trust your instinct. "

Flower Arrangement

After angering the untouchables

And receiving the refusal of the teacher,

I wonder:

        Am I the wrong one?

Maybe I should change poetics.

My poetry, then,

would cease to be this crown of thorns

that with burning verses offends the Despot.

Instead I will describe a beautiful arrangement with lilies.

That way, perhaps I will be forgiven

and someday they will embed me in the Official Anthology,

just like someone who would fit in a coffin

in the family crypt.

Etruscan Venus

It is only a fancy Etruscan statuette,
made of bronze.

She does not give, to whom looks at it,
the Roman voluptuousness;
her difficult beauty, with slender strokes,
requires preparation, sensitivity.

She does not breastfeed little calves.
Her short breasts
feed my songs.

Beauty Salon

You could own
an enviable body,
such as those living in the museums
of Rome, Madrid, New York.

In the mirror room of my poem
you would contemplate a complexion without wrinkles.
Or perhaps you think, naive one, that the face and body
of *La Maja* belonged to a single woman?,
Or that the Venus of the Quattrocento adhered
              to a diet?
Or that the skin of Aphrodite
              was of polished marble?

Listen: those artists retouched their models
because with them they shared
              tablecloth and sheets.

Come on, give me your body
and from here you will leave, I guarantee it,
physically satisfied.

Couple of Anthologists

Victoricus, better anthologist than poet,
better cuckold than anthologist,
is boiling: he debutes with horns,
and like the crazy blind man who distributes blows
he gives me one: he does not include me
in his new selection of authors.

You judge wrong, Victoricus: I was never
              on your lady's plate:
I am not part of her vast
and generous anthology.

My Friends Are Quiet

My friends do not read poetry,
                not even mine
nor that written by Propertius twenty centuries ago,
in spite of them being the sap of my verses,
in spite of my work being a mirror that conceals
                their imperfections.
In spite of that, they prefer
to touch the photos of *Cosmopolitan*
and find themselves in the celluloid mirror.
Next to the family fat one, the novel,
silence obscures the covers of my books.

Do my verses move you, oh cultured, sensitive Muse?
I really appreciate it, but I did not write them thinking
of you, but of those beautiful banal women.

Black Ink Brooch

She kidnapped me at the worst time.
Now I know why everyone hates her.
Inflexible, the Grim Reaper
did not allow me to assemble the last line,
black ink brooch, sealing, epitaph.

What Will my Readers Think?
Critics will throw projectiles
on this imperfect piece.

The lapidaries will frustrate their work
of chiseling a last line.
Some editorial house will cheat when it announces:
Anonymous, *Complete Works*.

If I had been on time to the reading of my palm
or if I had checked the horoscope of the day.

My widow does not stop crying.

As much as I tickle her sleeping feet, she does not respond.

I write telegrams to her, but the words get diluted

when she opens her eyes.

If my wife, instead of authorizing the editors

this lame piece-not an octet-

she would consult a *medium*,

I could dictate to her that damned verse

of which I begin to lose some detail,

but she never gave credit to charlatans.

Pity, my God, let me add that verse to my work,

it is not very long and is corrected,

and for it I would be remembered, I assure you.

Gorostiza, Juana Inés, Villaurrutia

and other colleagues advise me to forget it,

that is not worth it:

"words are blown away by the wind."

They look unconcerned, even happy.

It is understood: they are already immortal.

Héctor Carreto

Photo: Juan Miranda

ABOUT THE AUTHOR

Héctor Carreto (Mexico City, 1953) is a poet, translator and editor. His work has been widely published in several national and international magazines, and his poetry has been translated to English, French and Hungarian. He has served as a collaborator and editor of many magazines and newspapers such as Alforja, Casa del Tiempo, El Cocodrilo Poeta, La Jornada Semanal, Plural, and Tragaluz, among others. The present book, *Coliseum*, was the winner of the Aguascalientes National Poetry Prize in 2002, one of the most important poetry prizes in Mexico. He was a member of the National System of Art Creators (SNCA) from 2001 to 2007 and a fellow of the National Institute of Fine Arts (INBA / FONAPAS) in poetry, 1978. Currently he is a professor at the Autonomous University of Mexico City (UACM). He has published the following poetry books: *¿Volver a Ítaca?* (UNAM, 1979) *Naturaleza muerta* (UAM-A, 1980), *La espada de San Jorge* (Premiá, 1982), *Habitante de los parques públicos* (Conaculta (luz azul), 1992), *Incubus* (plaquette) (UAM, 1993), *Antología desordenada* (Conaculta/ICA (los cincuenta), 1996),

Coliseo (Joaquín Mortiz / Planeta, 2002), *El poeta regañado por la musa: antología personal* (Almadía, 2006), *Poesía portátil* 1979-2006 (UNAM, 2009) and *Clase turista* (Posdata editores, 2012).

ABOUT THE TRANSLATOR

Elvia Ardalani is a Professor of Spanish and Creative Writing in the Department of Writing and Language Studies at the University of Texas-Rio Grande Valley. Her work has appeared in different anthologies in the United States, Mexico and Spain. She has published the following poetry books: *El ser de los enseres, Callejón Kashaní, Cuadernos para un huérfano, Miércoles de Ceniza, De cruz y media luna/From Cross and Crescent Moon, Y comerás del pan sentado junto al fuego*, and Por *recuerdos viejos, por esos recuerdos.* She co-edited the volume *Miguel Hernández desde América* by published by the Fundación Cultural Miguel Hernández in Orihuela, Spain and The University of Texas-Pan American Press. She has translated to Spanish and English the poetry of Jalal al-Din Rumi, Omar Khayam, Elizabeth Bishop and others, as well as the works of some contemporary poets like Héctor Carreto, Vicente Quirarte and René Rodríguez Soriano. Her first novel, *El sótano del caracol*, is in the process of publication.

TABLE OF CONTENTS

I

Inscription 9

The Birth of Venus 10

Circus 11

The *Trojan* Horse 12

The Two Maecenas 13

Caligula's Son in Law 14

Caligula's Horse 15

Delikatessen 16

She 18

Coliseum 20

The Oldest Rat 22

Nightmare 23

Gymnasium 24

Burning the Eternal City 25

The Alley of Miracles 27

The Obelisk 28

Virtual Reality 29

Honors to Bacchus 30

Love Sickness   31

Drunkenness   32

Twin Peaks   33

Cronos   34

Cyclops   35

Mythology   36

II. Funeral Occasion

In the Tomb of Helen   41

The Blind   42

The Return   43

Offer   44

A Tomb Without Inscription   45

Forever Cinderella   46

Petition   47

Urns   48

Leonidas   49

Democracy   50

Octavius Epitaph   51

With Novenius, in the Republic of the Dead   52

III. Satellites

The Conquest of Space   57

Astronaut Warning   59

From the Moon, the Emperor Confesses   60

IV. Infections

My Poem, that Beast   65

Masterpieces   66

The Site of Troy   68

Infections   70

Dante Points Out   71

The Poet Scolded by the Muse   72

Flower Arrangement   74

Etruscan Venus   75

Beauty Salon   76

Couple of Anthologists   78

My Friends are Quiet   79

Blank Ink Brooch   80

Other **Poetry Books** in Libros Medio Siglo

Eyes Already Ruined – Luis Aguilar

Reduced to Dust – Luis Vicente de Aguinaga

The Being of the Household Beings – Elvia Ardalani

The Drunkenness of God – Luis Armenta Malpica

Huntings – Oliverio Arreola

In a Lute – The Cathedral – Silvia Eugenia Castillero

The Transfigured Heart – Dolores Castro Varela

Something Pains the Wind – Dolores Castro Varela

Theory of Losses – Jesús Ramón Ibarra

The Invincible – Vicente Quirarte

I Never Wanted to Stop Time – Sara Uribe

www.ingramcontent.com/pod-product-compliance
Lightning Source LLC
Chambersburg PA
CBHW051700040426
42446CB00009B/1223